Ms. Loops presents...

Handwriting Clues Club Books

Book 1
Clues to Find in Cursive & Print

Book 2
A-Z Dictionary of Clues

Book 3
A-Z Clues of Iggy... as found by Peony

Join the Handwriting Clues Club of adventurous people who become clues finders!

Ms. Loops Presents...

Handwriting Clues Club – Book 1
Clues to Find in Cursive & Print

by Judy Kaplan
(aka Ms. Loops)

Drawing of Ms. Loops by
Wayne Ramirez

Information for this work was gathered from professional
handwriting analysis sources. Efforts were made to assure
information accuracy. The author is not liable for differing
opinions that may arise.

Drawing of Ms. Loops by Wayne Ramirez.

Printed by KDP - https://kdp.amazon.com
ISBN: 978-1-957373-00-3 (Paperback)
ISBN: 978-1-957373-02-7 (Mobi)

Printed by Ingram Sparks - https://www.ingramspark.com
ISBN: 978-1-957373-09-6 (Hardback)
ISBN: 978-1-957373-01-0 (Epub)

Library Catalog Dewey Classification # - 155.2'82
Kaplan, Judy.
1. Graphology   2. Writing   3. Handwriting Analysis
I. Title.   II. Series.   III. Wayne Ramirez, illustrator

Judy Kaplan Books

JudyKaplanBooks.com

Acknowledgements

Thank you to the highly knowledgeable and professional handwriting analysts at these organizations:

American Handwriting Association Foundation
ahafhandwriting.org
American Association of Handwriting Analysts
aahahandwriting.org
International Grapho-Analysis Association
igas.com

Your courses, workshops, certification programs, and mentoring have been a thorough and enlightening education in handwriting analysis.

Thank you Linda Larson for your remarkably detailed evaluation of the information in this book.

Thank you to my family and friends for their incredible support, encouragement and patience throughout my writing.

Thank you to Wayne Ramirez for his wonderful depictions of my characters Ms. Loops, Iggy & Peony.

Author Information

Judy Kaplan has held a life-long fascination for writing, handwriting, and books. After a 27 year career as a High School Library Media Specialist, she began a second career as a Handwriting Analyst. She has Handwriting Analyst Certifications from both ahafhandwriting.org and igas.com. She specializes in personality and compatibility profiles. She created the Handwriting Clues Club series of books to promote understanding and compatibility in an easy, fun, and informative format for all ages.

Chapter 1

Welcome to the Handwriting Clues Club

Every handwriting has clues. Now that you joined my Handwriting Clues Club by opening this book, you will see how to find those clues.

I'm Ms. Loops. *I'm Ms. Loops.*

I will show you clues in both print and cursive. You can write print, cursive, or a mix of both. I prefer cursive because connecting letters is faster. Also for faster, I suggest a loose grip by thumb and pointer with the pen resting on the middle finger like this:

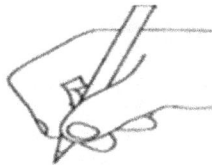

The more relaxed your grip, the easier it is to write.

To learn clues, it helps to know these letter parts.

GLOSSARY
of letter parts

Letters have zones-

Head Zone ➤dg is also called the ascender or the thinking zone. This part of the letter shows how a person thinks.

Body Zone ➤dg◄ is also called the x-height $\overline{X}\updownarrow$ or the practical zone. This part of the letter shows how a person interacts with others and manages their practical matters.

Leg Zone dg◄ is also called the descender or the action zone. This part of the letter shows how a person carries out the actions of getting things done.

Baseline - the ↓real line↓ or ↓imaginary line↓ that letters are written on. The baseline is a person's home-base of what's familiar and comfortable to them. The closer they write on the line, the more they want to stay close to what's familiar and comfortable.

Backbone or also called Stem - the tall line that supports the rest of the letter:

⬍E ⬍I ⬍H ⬍K ⬍T ⬍A ⬍Z ⬍b d⬍ ⬍f ⬍h ⬍k

Arm or Leg - a line attached to the Backbone.
Arms are: E⬅ F⬅ K←k←   Legs are: E↙ K↙k↙

Legs are also the descenders below the baseline g̅y̅ ◄

Crossbar - the line that crosses a Stem:

f← t← T↖ or connects two Stems: A← H←

t← Crossbar on t is also called a t-bar.

Swash - an extended decorative stroke on a letter:

↱A ↱M ↱Y

Flourish - a swirly showy stroke: ↘ₒA ↘ₒN↖ ℒ↙

Graphology - the study of handwriting analysis.
People who use handwriting clues to analyze handwriting on a ransom note for the police, or for a company to choose the best person for a job, or to help anyone better understand themselves or others, are called Graphologists.

Now let's look at HANDWRITING CLUES!

Chapter 2
Handwriting Clues Make Common Sense

Comfortable vs Uncomfortable to Read

Comfortable to read is the clue that they generally feel comfortable inside.

uncomfortable to read Uncomfortable to read
is the clue that they generally feel uncomfortable inside.

Steady vs *Bouncy*
Steady writing is the clue that their mood stays steady.

Bouncy writing is the clue that their mood bounces up & down

(Bouncy writing is the clue that their mood bounces up & down.)

Clear vs CONFUSED

Clear space between letters is the clue that they can think clearly.

OVERLAPPING Overlapping letters is the clue that their thinking is CONFUSED confused.

Big vs Small

Big writing is the clue that they want Big Attention. Big writers like others watching them.

Small writing is the clue that they only want small attention. Small writers like to be left alone.

MATCHING QUIZ:

1. Who feels more comfortable inside?

___ Comfortable ___ uNcoMFoRTableV

2. Whose mood bounces up and down?

___ Steady ___ Bouncy

3. Whose thinking is confused?

___ Clear ___ CONFUSED

4. Who wants more attention?

___ Big ___ Small

Chapter 3
Slant Shows Self-Control of Feelings

↑ vertical slant is straight up & down ↓

↗ right slant leans right ↗

↖ left slant leans left ↖

The vertical slant clue shows this person:

Keeps their feelings under control.

(Keeps their feelings under control.)

Stays objective and calm.

Won't show if they are upset or angry

(Won't show if they are upset or angry.)

Makes rational decisions in emergencies.

The right slant clue shows this person:

Leans towards other people.

(Leans towards other people.)

Is quickly friendly & interested in others.

Shows their upset feelings.

(Shows their upset feelings.)

Comforts others when they are upset.

Far right slant clue shows this person:

Leans too far on others. (Leans too far on others.)

Can't control their feelings.

Gets upset fast. (Gets upset fast.)

Needs a lot of calming down.

The left slant clue shows this person:

Leans back from others. (Leans back from others.)

Controls their feelings by holding them back.

Avoids talking about their feelings and personal life.

Is more comfortable talking about others.

Feels hurt and protects themselves from more hurt.

The far left slant clue shows this person:

Feels controlled by their past. (Feels controlled by their past.)

Controls their feelings by staying alone when they can.

Can seem friendly but won't talk about themselves.

Has trouble trusting anyone.

The variable slant clue shows this person:

Has feelings that shift a lot.

Is moody and unpredictable.

Many big slant shifts show they can't control their feelings.

Small slant shifts show small shifts in feelings that they can usually control.

Sometimes a *right slant* is given to a name, activity, or object as a clue that it is strongly liked.

Hey *Bestie,*
I love roller *skating* with you.
Your BFF,
Me

Sometimes a left slant is given to a name, activity, or object as a clue that it is strongly disliked:

Hey Meanie,
I never want to get yelled at again!
Your Upset Classmate,
Me

MATCHING QUIZ:

1. Who has a hard time trusting others?

2. Who is moody and unpredictable?

3. Who controls their feelings even in an emergency?

4. Who shows they care right away?

5. Who gets upset fast?

6. Who avoids talk about their feelings?

7. Who has feeling shifts they can usually control?

_____ *far right slant*

_____ vertical slant

_____ left slant

_____ *far left slant*

_____ big slant shifts

_____ **small slant shifts**

_____ *right slant*

Chapter 4

Thinking Space can be Clear or Confused

CONFUSEDSPACE:

The clue of no clear space between letters shows the
person is CONFUSED (confused).

Another clue that the person is unable to think clearly and
feels confused is OVERLAPPING (overlapping) letters.

They don't have enough clear thinking space and
can't make clearly thought out decisions.

Their decisions are based on their
confused feelings, not clear thinking.

Clear space between letters is the clue that
shows a person thinks clearly for themselves.

They see choices clearly and come to
well thought out decisions.

(They see choices clearly and come to well thought out decisions.)

Their clear thinking gives them confidence
in their decisions.

Too much thinking space between
letters is the clue that shows
thoughts don't stay connected.
This person:

*Needs lists to keep
their thoughts
connected* .

(Needs lists to keep their thoughts connected.)

Also can't easily connect to people
and prefers to be alone.

Space inside letters can be
narrow or open or wide.
These clues show how many choices the person
considers for their decisions.

The clue of narrow inside space is called narrow-minded.
This person considers only 1 or 2 choices for decisions.

The clue of open inside space is
called open-minded.
They consider a few choices for decisions.

Wide inside space is called
broad-minded. They consider
many choices for decisions.

MATCHING QUIZ:

1. Who has trouble keeping thoughts connected?

2. Who thinks clearly to decide what to do?

3. Whose thoughts are confused?

4. Who only considers 1 or 2 choices?

5. Who considers several choices?

6. Who considers a few choices?

___ clear letter space

___ too much letter space

___ CONFUSED SPACE

___ Narrow inside space

___ open inside space

___ broad inside space

Chapter 5
Pressure holds Memory, Energy & Feelings

There are 3 kinds of pressure:
Heavy, Moderate & *Light*

Heavy Pressure

A heavy press on paper makes a deep dent on the back of the page. Clues for this person are:

Has a strong, long lasting memory.
(Has a strong, long lasting memory.)

Has lots of physical energy and likes a lot of physical work.

Has a forceful personality that is quick to confront others & always wants their own way.
(Has a forceful personality that is quick to confront others and always wants their own way.)

Has strong senses that feel joy & hurts extra deeply.

They never forget and have a difficult time forgiving.
(They never forget and have a difficult time forgiving.)

They challenge themselves with lots of hard work.

Moderate Pressure

A moderate press on paper makes a small dent on the back of the page. Clues for this person are:

Has a good memory. (Has a good memory.)

Has good physical energy for moderate physical activity.

Prefers discussion over conflict.
(Prefers discussion over conflict.)

With good reason they forgive and forget.

They adapt well to changing situations.

Light Pressure

A light press on paper makes no dent on the back of the page. Clues for this person are:

Has a light memory that forgets easily
(Has a light memory that forgets easily.)

Has low physical energy and a gentle personality.

Needs to read facts many times to remember them.
(Needs to read facts many times to remember them.)

Prefers sitting activities to physical ones.

Avoids conflict and competition.
(Avoids conflict and competition.)

Easily forgives and forgets.

A FELT MARKER looks like heavy pressure
but there is no dent on the page.

Clues of a felt marker are any of these:

This person may want to look bigger than they feel.
(This person may want to look bigger than they feel.)

They may want to appear to work harder than they do.

They may also like the artistic look or
the smooth feel of markers.

MATCHING QUIZ:

1. Who always wants to avoid an argument?

2. Who prefers discussion over conflict?

3. Who has lots of energy and a long lasting memory?

4. Who may want to look bigger than they feel?

___ Heavy pressure

___ Light Pressure

___ Moderate Pressure

___ Felt Marker

Chapter 6
Baseline Focus can be Straight or Bouncy

Baseline is the ↓real line↓ or ↓imagined line↓
that letters are written on.

Baseline of the writing can
be straight,
have gentle bounces,
or have big bounces.

The clue of straight writing on baseline shows that person:

Keeps a straight focus on their work
(Keeps a straight focus on their work.)

Dislikes interruptions.

Ignores distractions. (Ignores distractions.)

If important to them, they will complete their task.

The clue of gentle bounces on the baseline shows that person:

Has a flexible focus. (Has a flexible focus.)

Gets distracted then easily returns to task.

Accepts interruptions as fine.

The clue of big bounces on the baseline shows that person:

Has a hard time staying focused.
(Has a hard time staying focused.)

Gets easily distracted by nearby sounds and activity.

Can't complete many of their tasks.

MATCHING QUIZ:

1. Who is very easily distracted?

2. Who doesn't like interruptions?

3. Who gets distracted but can get back on task?

___ gentle bounces on baseline

___ big bounces on baseline

___ straight on baseline

Chapter 7

Slope Attitude is Straight, Up or Down
Slope clues follow the baseline.

Baseline that goes straight across shows
a realistic attitude. This person:
Looks at what's realistic and practical.
Believes if they work hard they will reach
their goals.
Stays focused on their goals.
Keeps working towards them as much
as practical.

Baseline that slopes up shows
an optimistic attitude. This person:
Looks at the upside of every situation.
Believes bad situations will get better.
Believes hard work to reach goals is
always worth it.
Feels the joys in everyday life.
Makes others feel better with their
optimistic comments.

Baseline that slopes down can show
any of these 3:
1. A person's hand or whole body is physically
   tired. This is more common in children,
   especially after they are writing for a while.
2. The person has a pessimistic attitude and
   often looks at the downside of situations.
   They believe things usually get worse.
3. The person often feels generally down and
   sad. They are usually tired and have very
   little physical energy to get things done.

MATCHING QUIZ:

1. Whose attitude focuses on the upside of situations?

2. Whose attitude focuses on the downside of situations, or feels tired or sad?

3. Whose attitude focuses on the realistic side of situations?

___ baseline straight across

___ baseline slopes up

___ baseline slopes down

Chapter 8
Zone Size shows Where Attention Goes

Letters have 3 different zones:

Head zone (also called upper zone) ↗d↗f↖
is about a person's thinking.

Body zone (also called middle zone) →defg←
is about a person's practical planning & interactions.

Leg zone (also called lower zone) ↘g↗y↙
is about a person's physical-doing action.

The clues are in the size of the zone.
The person's biggest zone shows where
most of their attention goes.

Head zone is biggest clue shows that most of their
attention is on the ideas they like to think about.

Body zone is biggest clue shows that most of their attention
is on their everyday practical tasks and social life.

Leg zone is biggest clue shows that most of their attention
is on physically doing an activity and on getting things done.

Each zone can be tall, moderate, or short.

Head zone size ↗d̶f̶↖ is the clue that shows how much time a person spends on thinking theoretical ideas. Theoretical ideas are topics with several possible answers that people debate. They don't have one single answer that everyone accepts. Examples of theoretical ideas are issues and theories involving outer space, philosophy, politics or religion.

Tall head zone size is double the x-height. The clue of Tall Head shows the person:

Easily grasps and understands theoretical ideas.
(Easily grasps and understands theoretical ideas.)

Likes to spend a lot of time thinking about theoretical ideas.

Is easily more idealistic than practical.

Extra Tall head zone size is more than triple x-height
The clue of Extra Tall head shows the person:

Has strong beliefs & ideas that are made up theories far from reality.

Seems to have their head in the clouds.
(Seems to have their head in the clouds.)

Has unrealistically high standards & expectations for themselves and others.

Moderate head zone size is equal to the x-height.
The clue of moderate head zone shows the person:

Spends some time thinking about theoretical ideas.

Easily understands theoretical ideas if interested.
(Easily understands theoretical ideas if interested.)

Is mostly interested in theoretical ideas
with a practical purpose.

Short head zone size is shorter than x-height.
The clue of short head zone shows that person:

Doesn't spend time thinking about theoretical ideas.

Has a hard time understanding theoretical ideas.
(Has a hard time understanding theoretical ideas.)

Believes theoretical ideas are a waste of time.

Sticks to thinking only about what directly
affects them personally.

MATCHING QUIZ:

1. Who spends a lot of time thinking about theoretical ideas?

2. Who is mostly interested in theoretical ideas with a practical purpose?

3. Who has a hard time understanding theoretical ideas?

4. Who seems to have their head in the clouds?

___ Extra tall head zone

___ Tall head zone

___ Moderate head zone

___ Short head zone

Size of the body zone (also called middle zone) → *defg*
is the clue that shows how much of their attention
a person spends on their practical everyday life.
This includes everything practical they plan for home,
school, work, and social interactions with others.
Body zone size also shows how much attention
a person wants others to spend on them.

Tall body zone size is when the body zone is taller than the
head and leg zones. Tall body zone clue shows that person:

Gives most of their time & attention to practical matters.

Focuses on their daily needs & social plans.
(Focuses on their daily needs & social plans.)

Wants a lot of attention from others.

Moderate body zone is when the body zone is about the same
height as the head and leg zones. This clue shows that person:

Shares their time between their practical tasks & personal interests.

*Is good at making practical plans for
their ideas and everyday matters.*
(Is good at making practical plans for their ideas and everyday matters.)

Enjoys attention from others but doesn't feel it's necessary.

Short body zone is when the body zone is much smaller than the head and leg zones. Short body zone clue shows that person:

Spends very little time on practical matters and needs others to do their practical tasks.
(Spends very little time on practical matters and needs others to do their practical tasks.)

Has a very hard time making practical plans to put their ideas into action.

Is not interested in attention from others.
(Is not interested in attention from others.)

ALL BODY ZONE IS ALL LETTERS HAVE THE SAME HEIGHT.

LEG & HEAD ZONES ARE NOT USED IN THIS KIND OF WRITING.

ALL BODY ZONE CLUE SHOWS THIS PERSON IS:

ALL PRACTICAL, FOCUSED ON THEIR DAY TO DAY ROUTINES AND SOCIAL INTERACTIONS.

WANTS THEIR MESSAGE COMPLETELY CLEAR TO OTHERS.

ALL EXTRA BIG CAPITAL LETTERS
THIS CLUE SHOWS THEY WANT
A LOT OF ATTENTION.

MATCHING QUIZ:

1. Who needs a practical person to do their practical tasks?

2. Who is good at making practical plans for their ideas and everyday matters?

3. Who gives most of their time and attention to practical matters?

4. Who is all practical, focused on their day to day routines and social interactions?

5. Who wants a lot of big attention?

___ Short body zone

___ Moderate height body zone

___ Tall body zone

___ aLL BODY ZONe

__ EXTRA BIG CAPITAL LETTERS

Size of the leg zone (also called lower zone) ↳ _gry_

is the clue that shows how much time a person spends
actively *doing* a task. It can be actively doing a
physical task or actively doing sitting work.

Short leg zone is when the legs are very short.
This clue shows that person:

Only spends short periods of time actively doing their task.

Gets bored easily and gives up quickly
(Gets bored easily and gives up quickly.)

Has little interest in physical activity.

Moderate leg length is when the legs are about
the same height as moderate body height.
This clue shows that person:

Can work steadily for a few hours, then needs a break.
(Can work steadily for a few hours, then needs a break.)

Likes tasks that can be completed in a reasonable time
like a day, week, or possibly a month.

Enjoys some physical activity as part of their life.

Long leg length is when the legs are about twice the length of the body. This clue shows that person:

Works long amounts of time, determined to finish no matter how long it takes.
(Works long amounts of time, determined to finish no matter how long it takes.)

Works months or years on a project if important to them.
(Works months or years on a project if important to them.)

May do other people's tasks also.

Enjoys a lot of physical activity.

Very long leg is when the legs are more than 3 times the length of the body. This clue shows that person:

Likes spending lots of time physically actively doing.
(Likes spending lots of time physically actively doing.)

Is often restless and feels better when they change what they see.

Is always ready to change decor or travel to another place.
(Is always ready to change decor or travel to another place.)

MATCHING QUIZ:

1. Who feels better when they change what they see?

2. Who can work steadily for a while but then needs a break?

3. Who is determined to finish no matter how long it takes?

4. Who gets bored and gives up quickly?

___ Short leg length

___ Moderate leg length

___ Long leg length

___ Very long leg length

Chapter 9

t-bars Show Goal Height

$\uparrow$ high goals - $\dagger$ middle-height goals - $+$ low goals

t-bars high on the stem show they set high goals. They take a chance on hard goals that take a long time and a lot of hard work to reach.

t-bars in the middle of the stem show they set practical goals that take some work but they are sure they can reach in a practical amount of time.

Low t-bars on the stem show they set low goals. These are easy goals that take a short time to reach.

MATCHING QUIZ:

1. Who sets high goals?
2. Who sets middle-height goals?
3. Who sets low goals?

___ $+$

___ $\dagger$

___ $\uparrow$

Chapter 10
Lines are Straight Logic or Curvy Feelings

Straight lines → are the clue that shows
thinking with a straight logical plan.

Curvy lines ∿ are the clue that shows
thinking with curvy waves of feelings.

All writing has both

straight → and curvy ∿ lines.

The clue of mostly straight lines shows that person:

Thinks mostly with logic, not slowed down
by intruding feelings.

Likes being in charge.
(Likes being in charge.)

Argues rather than bends to
what others want.

The clue of mostly curves shows that person:

Thinks mostly with feelings, which takes much time to sort through to make decisions

Is friendly and patient.

(Is friendly and patient.)

Bends to what others want rather than argue.

The clue of lots of both straight and curved lines shows that person:

Makes decisions based on both logic and feelings.

Finds a friendly way to be in charge.

(Finds a friendly way to be in charge.)

Discusses their point and wants a friendly solution.

Backbones, also called stems, can be straight or bending.

The clue of firm, straight backbones $E $h
shows the person stands up for themselves and their beliefs.
They have a firm backbone and don't give in
to pressure from others.

The clue of bending backbones g↞ ↠h
Shows the person gives in instead of
standing up for themselves and their beliefs.
They cave-in to pressure from others

(The clue of bending backbones shows the person gives-in instead of standing
up for themselves and their beliefs. They cave-in to pressure from others.)

Writing that is all thready has no backbone or exact form.
It looks like thread and can't be read.

(If some is thready and it's mostly readable, that's done to write faster.)

——————— or ∿∿∿∿∿

The clue of all unreadable thready writing shows the person:

Does not take a firm stand on any beliefs.

Bends to the beliefs of those around them.

Does not want responsibility or commitments.

Chooses the easiest way to do things.

MATCHING QUIZ:

1. Who discusses their point and wants a friendly solution?

2. Who argues rather than gives in to others?

3. Who is friendly and patient?

4. Who stands firm in their beliefs?

5. Who wants no responsibility and no commitments?

6. Who gives in instead of standing up for themselves or their beliefs?

___ mostly curves

___ Lots of both straight and curved lines

___ mostly straight Lines

___ ～～～～～

___ bending backbone

___ Firm straight backbone

Chapter 11

Loops Hold Imagination & Feelings

Big loops are clues that show inflated imagination and feelings that are uncomfortably big.

Daydreamer Head 𝓛 𝓛

Inflated head zone loops show they have so much imagination and so many feelings going on at once, they easily get lost in fantasies or daydreams. They are more involved with their own thoughts than what is going on around them. Their thinking is also constantly adding new thoughts. That makes it hard to decide on or stick to a decision. They are easily uncomfortably confused about what to do.

Sensitivity Loops 𝓭 & 𝓽

d & t loops show how a person evaluates themselves. The person with big d & t loops evaluates themselves to discomfort. They constantly criticize themselves and believe others constantly criticize them as well. They hear everything said to them as a criticism. The closed loop shows they keep these thoughts inside and don't show what they're feeling to others. Many people with sensitivity loops use their self criticisms to improve their work. The perspective they choose, to feel bad or improve, is up to them.

Worry Loops ᴍ ɴ ʀ

m, n & r don't usually have loops. When a person adds body zone loops that point down like these ↓m ↓n ↓r, it shows the person holds onto uncomfortable feelings of worry. The person worries even when there's no actual reason. They imagine problems beyond what's practical and cautious. They waste a lot of time and energy on worrying. They turn a problem over and over in their mind in a troubled way. If the writing has many worry loops, it shows their worry affects them often. A few worry loops shows they feel it sometimes.

Bluffing Loops ℬ 𝓂 ℛ

Inflated loops beginning a capital show a person has uncomfortable feelings that they don't have the abilities they need. The closed loop shows they want to hide that feeling from others. To hide that feeling they inflate their abilities in the eyes of others by bluffing. Bluffers are able to speak easily and sound impressive. While they pretend to have strong abilities, they still feel uncomfortably inadequate inside.

Money Bags g ɟ y

Inflated leg zone loops show the person rates their self worth by their physical possessions or accomplishments they can show to others. The big loop also shows the amount of actions or accomplishments they expect of themselves. Since the loops are overly large, it shows they expect to possess or accomplish more than is possible. They feel the discomfort of never possessing enough or of never doing enough. They may have or do plenty, but the big loop shows they feel an empty inside hole that they can't seem to fill.

MATCHING QUIZ:

1. Who has worry loops showing worry for no reason?

2. Who has bluffing loops and is good at pretending their abilities are better than they really are?

3. Who has sensitivity loops that show they constantly feel criticized?

4. Who has money bags showing how many possessions or accomplishments they need to feel good self worth?

5. Who has daydreamer head and is more involved in their own thoughts than what's going on around them?

— ꝺ ꝺ ꝺ

___ 𝒬 & ⇡

___ ℬ 𝓂 ℛ

___ 𝓂 𝓃 𝓇

___ 𝒬 ℏ

Chapter 12

Body Circles show Honesty or Secrecy

Body zone clues show how a person interacts
with others in their everyday practical life.

Think of body zone circle letters a & o
as a person's mouth.

Open circle-mouths α υ is the clue that
shows their mouths are often open,
meaning they like to talk a lot.

Closed circle-mouths a o is the clue that
shows their mouths are often closed,
meaning they only talk when needed.

Body zone circles also hold the clues that show
what's on a person's mind when they talk.

Clear space inside the circle-mouths for both open or

closed - α υ or a o - is the clue that shows they speak
honestly with nothing hidden in their mind.

Closed loops inside the circles is the clue that shows they have thoughts they like to keep private. These can be personal thoughts for themselves only, or they can be secrets they keep involving themselves or others.

Small private thoughts or secrets a σ

Big private thoughts or secrets a σ

Very big loop inside the circle Q θ
is the clue that shows there are
big amounts of imagination and feelings
involved in their private thoughts.
If it's a secret, they imagine and fear the worst
if others were to find out what the secret is.

Overlapping loops a θ is the clue that shows one secret overlapping into another secret and blocking the person's clear thinking. The size of the overlap shows how much they feel they need to protect. A big overlap θ easily leads the person to tell a lie to protect that secret.

Hooks or lines inside a circle a or σ are a clue that shows the person has something in their mind that they avoid having to say. They may tell a little but avoid telling the whole truth about it.

MATCHING QUIZ:

1. Who has secrets that block their clear thinking?

2. Who has small private thoughts or secrets?

3. Who fears terrible things will happen if their big secrets are known?

4. Who likes to talk a lot?

5. Who avoids telling the whole truth of what's on their mind?

6. Who speaks honestly and only talks when they need to?

____ a ⊙

____ a ∪

____ ℓ ⊖

____ a σ

____ a ○

____ Q ⊘

Chapter 13

Angles are Sharp Thinking & Sharp Tongue

∧↑ angles that have a sharp point up are the clue
for curiosity to explore for more information.
This is sharp exploratory thinking to figure out *why*.

∨↓ angles that have a sharp point down are
the clue for an analytic mind that dives right into
problem solving. This is sharp analytic thinking.
Sharp analytic thinking is very quick to figure out
which information is useful and which is not.

Angles with a good amount of clear space
inside the angle like these
∧∧∧
have a good amount of thinking space
to make well thought out decisions.
This angle clue
∧∧∧
shows the person has Sharp & Clear thinking.

m is the easiest letter to see the thinking clues for

clear & curious ↑M /M↑ -or- clear & analytic ↓M м↓

Clues of curious sharp points up with clear
thinking space ↑M M↑ show the person:

Explores ideas for new possibilities.
Is always curious for new answers to 'Why?'

Clues of analytic sharp points down with clear thinking
space ↓M M↓ show the person is:
Quick to analyze a problem,

quick to see the solution, and then...

quick to state what they want done to solve it.

Some people take that quick statement of solution
as criticism and say that person has a
Sharp Critical Tongue.

Comments made by a Sharp Critical Tongue can be
heard as harsh criticism by some people. The person
with the sharp tongue would say they only mean it to
help. People with clear analytic thinking do have good
solutions for others to consider. A person with
sharp, clear thinking usually hears it as help.

Angles that don't have enough thinking space like these

show there is not enough thinking space for clear thinking. This clue shows the person is easily frustrated because they can't think clearly to make clear decisions. This person's:

many angles without clear thinking space shows quick to get frustrated....

(many angles without clear thinking space shows quick to get frustrated...)

and wanting to control whats done around them but they don't have clear thinking to make clear plans.

(and wanting to control what's done around them but they don't have clear thinking to make clear plans.)

While angles with clear thinking space shows curious & analytic thinking, too many angles does not make a person a better thinker.

Too many angles is a clue that the person quickly becomes impatient, which then can quickly turn to anger. Impatience, and certainly anger, take away from a person's ability to think clearly.

Writing that is mostly angles shows there is
a lot of impatience and anger inside the person.
The more angles, the more
impatience and anger there is.

Too many angles are clues that this person is:

Quick to argue

Won't ever change their mind

Must have their own way, and

Is easily frustrated

Writing with a mix of angles and curves
is the clue that their angles showing
impatience and anger –
are combined with curves
showing they also have
some amount of
gentle nature and patience.

People whose writing has many more
sharp, clear angles than gentle curves are:

Sharp quick thinkers.

Automatic problem solvers.

Quickly critical of what's wrong, and quickly
state their way to solve it.

Aggressive and hard working to get what they want.

They are also able to use the curves they have
for some gentle caring and patience.

A mix of more curves with some sharp angles
shows that person:

Likes challenges and solving them.

(Likes challenges and solving them.)

Is friendly while accomplishing tasks.

Considers feelings when making decisions.

MATCHING QUIZ:

1. Which person has a lot of anger and impatience inside of them?

2. Who does not have enough clear thinking space for clear thinking and is easily frustrated?

3. Who has clear thinking and can make clearly thought out decisions?

4. When a person writes with many down-pointed V-angles and is quick to criticize, what is it called?

5. Who likes challenges while they are also thoughtful of others?

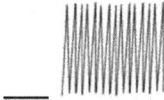

___ |||||||||||||||

___ /\/\/\/\/\/\/\

___ MOSTLY ANGLES

___ sharp critical tongue

___ more curves with some sharp angles

Chapter 14

Special Shapes are for Special Attention

i j – circles for dots is a clue that shows they want to be seen as creative and unique.

ï ÿ - Heart dots is a clue that shows they desire love and romance from others.

ie g – filled in closed shapes is a clue that shows they feel a heavy weight of sadness inside them.

→# – persistence loops are loops of feelings inside a person to prove to themselves that they can do it. This clue shows the person persists in pushing forward →#.

Snail curls ~ is a clue that shows they are wound up in themselves and can be selfish. They desire all attention on them.

Hooks on many letters — is a clue that shows a person is possessive. They strongly want to be noticed for all they possess. They also like the feel of holding things in their hands.

k p u- temper tics are short sharp angles at the beginning of any letter ⁊u.
This clue shows a quick temper.
Temper tics are a warning notice to others.

⋀ ⋀ — long lines at a sharp angle are a clue that the person feels a strong need to protect themselves. The angle shows there's an angry feeling behind it and the long line is their line of protection. This angle ╱ shows the source of the anger was in the past. They are adamant against letting it happen again. This angle ╲ shows protecting themselves from what could be said to them in the future. They are adamant against letting others attack their judgment or decisions.

MATCHING QUIZ:

1. Who wants to be seen as unique and creative?

2. Who desires love and romance from others?

3. Who feels a strong need to protect themselves?

4. Who holds heavy sad feelings inside?

5. Who has a quick temper?

6. Who has persistence to prove what they can do?

7. Who is wound up in themselves?

8. Who is possessive & likes the feel of holding things?

___ Snail curls

___ f H

___ k p u

___ M M

___ e g

___ Hooks on many letters

___ i j

___ i j

Chapter 15

Zones Push & Pull Uncomfortable Feelings

Legs pulled ←left is the clue that the person's actions
are pulled by feelings from their past when they
longed for more love and support.
Actions they do now are affected by still wanting
that love and support, now wanting it
from those presently around them.

Legs pushed right→ is the clue that the person takes
hurtful feelings from their past and pushes those bad
feelings into action to improve their future.

A firm push ↘ from body zone into legs zone shows
the person insists things are done their way.
They have put their foot down as the final word.
In truth, they insist they are right to protect their
lack of confidence that they might be wrong.

m ⁀n ⁀u

A firm push ↗ from legs zone into body zone shows the person feels resentment from actions that happened in their past. They hold grudges that continue to upset them. Those resentful feelings still bother them and make them snap at people even if they only suspect that person might do something that hurts them.

w ẋ y

A long pull ↘ from head zone into body zone shows the person feels their past accomplishments didn't get enough notice. They feel cheated from praise they feel they should have had.

V w X

A long push ↗ from the body zone into the head zone shows the person is ambitious and wants their future success noticed. They want to prove to others how successful they can be.

MATCHING QUIZ:

1. Who feels they didn't get enough love or support in their past?

2. Who pushes their energy into their work to improve their future?

3. Who puts their foot down insisting that things get done their way?

4. Who feels resentment at things that happened in their past?

5. Who feels their past accomplishments didn't get enough notice?

6. Who is ambitious and wants their future success noticed?

___ ᵷ ᵷ ᵞ

___ ᵈ ᴍ ᵡ

___ ᵐ ᶰ ᶬ

___ ᵛ ᵂ ᵡ

___ ᵂ ᵡ ᵞ

___ ᵞ ᵷ ᵡ

Chapter 16
Capitals show Self Esteem

Capitals Simple And Clear Are The Clue That The Person:

Is Comfortable With Who They Are.

(Is Comfortable With Who They Are.)

Is Efficient And Doesn't Waste Time.

Does Not Need Extra Attention.

Capitals 2-times as Tall as x-height Is The Clue That the Person:

Feels Confident In Their Abilities.

Has Good Self Esteem.

(Has Good Self Esteem)

Wants to Prove Accomplishments to Themselves More than to Others.

Capitals 3-times as Tall as x-height Is The
Clue That The Person:

Feels Small Inside But Wants To Be Treated Like A Bigshot.

Wants To Appear Larger Than They Feel.
(Wants to appear larger than they feel.)

Exaggerates Their Own Accomplishments.

Capitals Extra Fancy Is The Clue That They:

Want To Appear Extra Impressive.
(Want to Appear Extra Impressive.)

May Feel Inadequate As They Are.

Want To Be Remembered.
(Want To Be Remembered.)

Capitals Extra Small Is The Clue That They:

Are Modest About Themselves and their Accomplishments.
(Are modest about themselves and their accomplishments.)

Do Not Expect or Desire Extra Notice From Others.

MATCHING QUIZ:

1. What do Capitals Twice as Tall as x-height mean?

2. What do Capitals Simple and Clear mean?

3. What do Capitals Extra Large mean?

4. What do Capitals Extra Fancy mean?

5. What do Capitals Extra Small mean?

___ Feels Confident In Their Abilities.

___ Is Efficient And Doesn't Waste Time.

___ Wants To Appear Larger Than They Feel.

___ Wants To Be Remembered.

___ Does Not Expect or Desire Extra Notice From Others.

Chapter 17
Fear Factors to Find

fear of change clues show in:
(Fear of change clues show in:)

very narrow letters
(very narrow letters).

hugs tight to the baseline
(letters that hug tight to the baseline.)

Jealousy or fear of not being loved, clues show in:
(Jealousy or fear of not being loved clues show in:)

far left slant

beginning flat or tight loops ↗𝓂 ↗𝓂

sharp angles that point to upper left ↗𝓃 ↘w

Fear of criticism or disapproval clues show in:

inflated loops on *l* and/or *t*

light PRessURe

mostly curves

left slant and pulls to the left *y*

bottom hump to the left *↓g ↓y*

hidden thoughts in a person's mind *a o*

big private thoughts or secrets *a o*

overlapping private thoughts or secrets *a o*

MATCHING QUIZ:

1. What shows jealousy or fear of not being loved?

2. What shows fear of change?

3. What shows fear of criticism or disapproval?

___ very narrow letters

___ *m m*

___ *l* or *t*

Chapter 18

Signature Represents the Person

Everyone's handwriting is different. That makes a handwritten signature the perfect representation of that person. Signatures can be cursive, print, full name, initials, or an image. For people who can not write, it can be a mark like an X.

A handwritten full name signature is the hardest to imitate and the best for legal proof that it was written by that person. Simply written initials are easily imitated and can more easily be a forgery.

Hard to imitate and best protection against forgery:

My Unique Signature

My Unique Signature

Easy to imitate for a forgery:

ME

ME

Signatures also hold many clues about the person.

When a signature looks similar to the person's usual writing, it is the clue that the person wants to represent themselves as they are.

This is how I write.
My Signature

This is how I write.
My Signature

When a signature is very different from the person's usual writing, it is the clue they want to represent themselves to others with a very different image.

My Usual Writing

My Usual Signature

My Usual Writing
My Usual Signature

Signature that is much bigger than their usual writing is the clue for wanting to appear bigger than they feel.

This is how I write.

My Signature

Signature that is much smaller than their usual writing is the clue for wanting to avoid notice from others. They either prefer being left alone or they have low self esteem and feel unworthy of other people's notice.

This is how I write.
My Signature.

59

Signature that is initials is the clue that they don't want others to know everything about them.
This is all you get to know:

ms

ms

Signature that is unreadable is the clue that they don't want others to know anything about them.

Signature with extra added flourishes or swashes is the clue that they want to make an extra long-lasting impression on others.

Signature that's made with a particular image is the clue that they want to be known as that image.

Signature images could be:

People who write their signature many times a day
sometimes end up scribbling.

s ni nl ni n

This is done to be fast but also is a clue that they don't
want to spend time revealing themselves to the others.

The largest name written, or the name with the
largest first letter, shows which part of their
identity is most important to them.

First Middle Last

First Name Largest is the clue that they feel their
individual self is more important to their identity
than their family is.

First Middle Last

Middle Name Largest is the clue that they feel
their most personal hidden inner self is the
most important part of their identity.

First Middle Last

Last Name Largest is the clue that their family name
identity (could also be a step-family or married name) is
the most important part of their personal identity.

MATCHING QUIZ:

1. Who feels their family name is the most important part of their identity?

2. Who doesn't want to spend the time revealing themselves to others?

3. Who only wants others to know a little about them?

4. Who has a hard signature to forge?

5. Who wants to represent themselves with a very different image?

6. Who wants to be known for a drawn image?

7. Who doesn't want others to know anything about them?

8. Who wants to make an extra long-lasting impression on others?

9. Who wants to avoid notice from others?

10. Who wants to represent themselves just as they are?

___

___

___ First Middle Last

___ My signature

___ My Signature

___ This is how I write. My Signature.

___ MS

___ My Unique Signature

___ This is how I write. My Signature

___ My Usual Writing My Usual Signature

Chapter 19

Them vs You: Inevitable Conflicts

SLANT CONFLICT:

They write with a *far right slant.* They can't control their feelings and get upset fast.

You write with a **vertical slant**. You don't show your feelings and keep your feelings under control at all times.

They yell, "How can you be so cold, don't you feel how bad this is?"

You can mutter to yourself, 'Who wants to be hysterical like you?'

or...

You can say, "I know you think I'm cold because I don't show my feelings. I do feel upset for you. But my way is to step back and think it through so I see it from all sides. Tell me what you're feeling and then I'll tell you how I see it."

THINKING-SPACE CONFLICT:

They write with no thinking space between letters
NOTHINKINGSPACE. They can't think clearly or make a
well thought out decision.

You write with **clear *thinking space*** between letters.
You think clearly for yourself and can make well thought
out decisions.

They yell, "What's the matter with you? These flowers
are perfect to make my mother forget I broke her
grandmother's vase."

You can mutter to yourself, 'You must have just
swallowed your last brain cell.'

or...

You can say, "I know you want to make up with your
mom, but your mom loves looking at flowers and will
notice they're missing from your neighbor's garden.
Then she'll be mad at you for that also and it will be
even harder to make up with her. Do you see how that
will happen?"

PRESSURE CONFLICT:

They write with **heavy pressure**. They need a lot of physical activity and have a forceful manner.

You write with light pressure. You prefer sitting activities and have a gentle manner.

They yell, "You're so lazy, you can't even get off your butt for a game of hoops!"

You can mutter to yourself, 'You're nothing but a stupid jumping jack.'

or...

You can say, "I know you think I'm lazy because I'm not into physical activity like you, but I am interested in being a writer and learning what other people think. I'd really like to know what you like best about playing basketball. Will you tell me? And then I'd like to watch you play."

BASELINE CONFLICT:

They write with a <u>bouncy baseline</u>. They have a hard time staying focused and welcome any little distraction as an excuse to stop doing their task.

You write with a <u>straight baseline.</u> You stay focused and dislike distractions. You don't want to stop until you complete your task.

They yell, "This is taking too long, I need a break!"

You can mutter to yourself, 'Give me a break and just leave.'

or...

You can say, "I know you think I'm all work and no play, but I get uncomfortable if I stop before I'm done. I know you need breaks. How about you take a five minute break every 15 minutes. Can you set your alarm and do that for yourself?"

SLOPE CONFLICT:

They write with a baseline that slopes down. They are a pessimist who believes all situations only get worse. They feel it's a waste of time to try and give up fast.

You write with a baseline that slopes up. You are an optimist who believes that if you keep trying bad situations will certainly get better. You feel hard work is always worth it.

They yell, "This is bad and it's going to get worse, let's quit!"

You can mutter to yourself, 'If you keep complaining it's sure to get worse.'

or...

You can say, "I know you think I don't see how bad things are, but my experience tells me if I believe it will get better then I have a good chance of making it better. Will you help me give that a try this time?"

ZONES CONFLICT:

They write their letters with short heads. They see ideas that are theoretical and not practical as a waste of time.

You write your letters with tall heads. You like spending a lot of time thinking about theoretical ideas.

They yell, "Stop wasting time and do something worthwhile!"

You can mutter to yourself, 'You can't think beyond yourself to understand that it's ideas that change the world.'

or...

You can say, "I know you think my head is lost in the clouds. But what I'm doing is thinking about a way to make it better for people who are hungry around the world. Will you help me make signs for a fundraiser for the food bank?"

CURVES vs STRAIGHT LINES CONFLICT:

They write with **mostly straight lines**. They like sticking straight to what they planned to do and will argue rather than bend to what others want.

You write with **mostly curves**. You are most interested in pleasing others and prefer to bend to what others want rather than to argue.

They yell, "You should never have agreed to help them again. They take advantage of you."

You can mutter to yourself, 'You always complain when I help someone that's not you.'

or...

You can say, "I'm the kind of person who likes helping others. Is there something you need help with today?"

LARGE LOOPS CONFLICT:

They write with inflated leg loops g j y. They evaluate their self worth by how much money and how many possessions they have. They never feel they have enough.

You write with inflated Q and Y loops. You evaluate yourself by constantly imagining every criticism possible of yourself and every criticism others might have about you. You never feel good enough as you are. You always feel you need to do more to prove you are worthy of considering yourself good enough.

They yell, "You're crazy wasting all that time on writing poems that others will never see. Buy yourself that necklace you want, that will make you feel a lot better."

You can mutter to yourself, 'I can't do anything right in your eyes.'

or...

You can say, "I know you're trying to help. But I need to know for myself that I can fill a whole book with poems and feel good about it for myself without worrying what others will say. This is a challenge only for me to know if I can do it."

LOW GOAL vs HIGH GOAL CONFLICT:

They write low t-bars meaning they have low goals. They only want easy goals that don't take long to reach and have a sure result.

You write high T-bars meaning you have high goals. You are willing To take a chance on Trying to achieve a goal That Takes a long Time and a loT of hard work.

They yell, "All you do is practice the saxophone all day. When are you going to stop that and start doing something fun?"

You can mutter to yourself, 'If it's not super easy then it's too hard for you.'

or...

You can say, "I know you want to see that new movie and you've been waiting to see it with me. I appreciate that a lot. But I hope you can understand how much band means to me and how I want to get a music scholarship for college. Give me today to get better at this new marching tune and tomorrow we'll go to the movie together."

HONESTY vs SECRECY CONFLICT:

They write with clear circles a O. They speak honestly, not feeling they have anything to hide.

You write with big secrecy loops Q O. You're hiding what's on your mind and you have big feelings about it. You fear others won't understand and will criticize you if those private thoughts are known.

They yell, "You never tell me anything. Why don't you trust me?"

You can mutter to yourself, 'If I did tell you, you would think I was crazy or stupid and you would tell everyone you know how ridiculous I am.'

or...

You can say, "I know I keep things private and that to you it's wrong. But I'm so scared others won't understand. I need time to think about it more. Can you accept that about me?"

SHARP-TONGUE vs ANALYTICAL-SOLUTIONS
CONFLICT:

They write MANY ANGLES WITH NOT ENOUGH THINKING SPACE INSIDE THE ANGLES. They don't have enough thinking space to clearly figure things out. Also, the many angles show they get angry fast.

You write many angles with enough thinking space inside them to think clearly and analytically to solve problems. You enjoy the challenges of problems and solving them. You quickly offer a solution meant to help, though the other person hears your suggestions as a 'sharp critical tongue'.

They yell, "I tell you what's wrong and you get all mean telling me how I did everything wrong. I'm not wrong, you are!"

You can mutter to yourself, 'You have no idea what a walking disaster you are.'

or...

You can say, "I know this situation is frustrating for you and I really didn't mean to hurt you. I want to help by explaining how to see it. I'll write down the steps I think will solve this problem and you can read it if you want to. Will you accept that from me?"

SPECIAL SHAPES CONFLICT:

They write *lots of snail curls*. They are wound up in themselves, put their own needs first, and can be selfish.

You write *lots of hooks*. You are possessive and tenaciously hold onto what you want to possess or achieve, whether it's objects, people, or goals. You also like physically holding onto things in your hands.

They yell, "I didn't say you could hold my teddy bear!"

You can mutter to yourself, 'You're too selfish to share anything, that's why I didn't bother to ask.'

or...

You can say, "I know that teddy bear is important to you. But I always have this need to hold things and feel them in my hand. I should have asked. Can I hold it for a while?"

ACTION ZONE PULL vs PUSH CONFLICT:

They write many leg pulls to the left. They spend a lot of their action time thinking about hurtful feelings from their past.

You write many leg pushes to the right. You take hurtful feelings from your past and push those bad feelings into action to improve your future.

They yell, "I'm having a bad day, I can't get anything done. I'm giving up on this stupid project."

You can mutter to yourself, 'You're just lazy, I'm done with your excuses.'

or...

You can say, "I'm sorry you're having a bad day. I'd like to help you get started on that project. If we do it together it will get your mind off the bad stuff. Let's give it a try."

FEAR-OF-CHANGE vs FEAR-OF-DISAPPROVAL
CONFLICT:

They have very narrow writing. Narrow letters show they are narrow-minded in what they consider right or proper to do. They are only comfortable with what's familiar and fear any kind of change.

You write with large secret loops which shows you keep some thoughts private that you fear others won't understand or approve. You have fear of disapproval.

They yell, "You keep wanting me to try something that I don't do. And something like that is just not acceptable around here."

You can mutter to yourself, 'I can count on you to disapprove of everything I want to do. Why did I even ask?'

or...

You can say, "I know you are not comfortable with trying new things. But I think a new club at school for handwriting clues would be fun. Except I'm afraid everyone will think I'm crazy for suggesting it. I'd like to know your opinion. If you think it's fun then it's worth a try. Will you listen and tell me if any of it sounds like fun to you?"

XL-CAPITALS vs XS CAPITALS CONFLICT:

They write Extra Large Capitals. They feel small inside and want to appear larger than they feel. They easily exaggerate their own accomplishments and always desire a lot of admiration from others.

You write Extra Small Capitals. You are modest about yourself and your accomplishments. And you don't expect or desire extra notice from others.

They yell, "I just said we bowled 20 points higher than we did. What's the big deal?"

You can mutter to yourself, 'You can't ever stick to the truth. You'll never get that truth is bigger and matters more than both of us put together.'

or...

You can say, "I know you think it's fun to stretch the truth to make it sound bigger. But I'm a detail freak and to me the exact truth matters more than it does to you. I understand the way you see it. Do you want to understand how I see it?"

FIRST NAME BIGGER vs LAST NAME BIGGER
CONFLICT:

They write their signature with their first name bigger
Firstname Lastname. They feel their personal
identity is about them and them only. They do not feel
their own identity depends on their family or their
family name.

You write your signature with the first letter of your
last name bigger Firstname Lastname. You feel your
personal identity comes most importantly from your
family. It's your family name and family unit that is
what identifies you as who you are.

They yell, "When are you going to make your own
decisions? You always do what your family wants. Don't
be a doctor, grow up and make your own choice."

You can mutter to yourself, 'You have no plan for your
future, you're going to end up flipping greasy burgers.'

or...

You can say, "I know you think it's important to make
your own choices. But I don't know what I want to be.
Being a doctor like my mom feels like good footsteps to
follow. Do you want to help me look into what kinds of
doctors there are? Maybe you'll find a kind of doctor
you want to be and we can be doctors together?"

Chapter 20

Handwriting Clues Adventures Begin

Handwriting Clues Club
is happy to announce that your
Handwriting Clues Adventures
begin now!

Find the clues of:
*what's most important to you
*what's most important to those around you
*what's easy or hard for you
*what's easy or hard for those around you
*what are the kind of goals you want to achieve
*what are the kind of goals those around you want
*and how can you all understand each other better.

Great Clues Adventures to you...
Ms. Loops